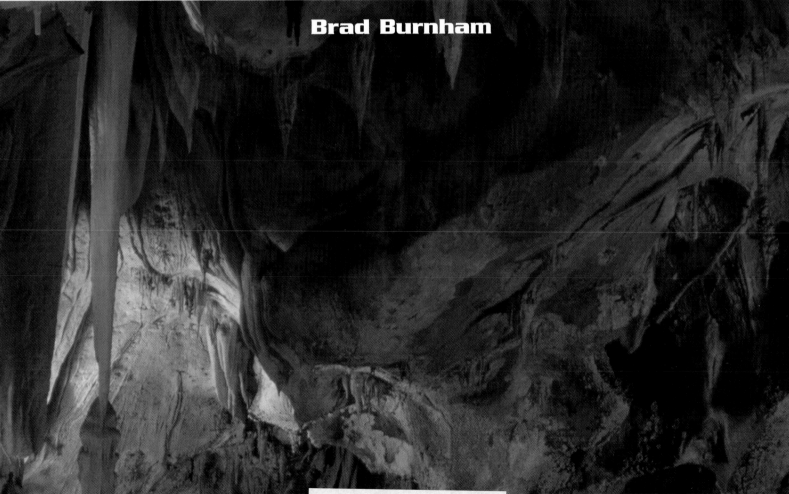

# Carlsbad Caverns

## America's Largest Underground Chamber

Brad Burnham

The Rosen Publishing Group's
PowerKids Press ™
New York

*For John and Jane*

Published in 2003 by The Rosen Publishing Group, Inc.
29 East 21st Street, New York, NY 10010

First Edition

Editor: Nancy MacDonell Smith
Book Design: Michael J. Caroleo and Michael de Guzman

Photo Credits: Cover, title page © Adam Woolfitt/CORBIS; pp. 4, 8, 12, 16, 19 © Michael Nichols/National Geographic; p. 7 courtesy of the National Park Service; pp. 11, 20 © Superstock; p. 15 © Chad Ehlers/International Stock Photo.

Burnham, Brad.
Carlsbad Caverns : America's Largest Underground Chamber / by Brad Burnham.— 1st ed.
    p. cm. — (Famous caves of the world)
Includes bibliographical references and index.
Summary: Introduces and explores the Carlsbad Caverns.
  ISBN 0–8239–6256–3
1.  Carlsbad Caverns (N.M.)—Juvenile literature. 2. Carlsbad Caverns National Park (N.M.)—Juvenile literature. [1. Carlsbad Caverns (N.M.)] I. Title. II. Series.
    F802.C28 B87 2003
    978.9'42–dc21

                                                          2001006023

Manufactured in the United States of America

# Contents

NEW MEXICO

Carlsbad
Caverns

# Carlsbad Caverns National Park

One of America's greatest treasures is found in the state of New Mexico. This treasure is underground. It is a series of connected underground caves, called **caverns**. The caverns were made through millions of years. They are part of Carlsbad Caverns National Park, which was created in 1930. This park includes the caverns and 46,766 acres (18,926 ha) of land above ground.

The walls, the floors, and the ceilings of Carlsbad Caverns are covered with beautiful rock formations. These were made through millions of years, too. Thousands of people visit Carlsbad Caverns every year to learn how the caverns were made and to see the beautiful rock formations.

*The largest room in Carlsbad Caverns covers 14 acres (6 ha).*

# The Curious Cowboy

Around 1900, a cowboy named Jim White was hired to work in the caves. With the light of his lantern, he saw many wonderful things. What he saw made him curious. He began to **explore** the caves. He loved what he saw and decided to share it with other people. White took many people to see the caverns.

In 1924, a team from *National Geographic* magazine came to see the caverns. Jim White was their guide. White showed the **geographers** the different caves. *National Geographic* published a story with pictures of the caverns for the whole world to see. The article described the caverns as "the most **spectacular** of underground wonders in America."

*Jim White (far right) was the person who brought Carlsbad Caverns to the public's attention. This photograph of him was taken in 1939.*

# The Making of the Caverns

About 250 million years ago, Carlsbad Caverns was not a series of caves but solid **limestone** rock at the bottom of an ocean. Limestone is a kind of rock made from the bodies of small ocean animals. After the ocean dried up, the limestone started to crack. Water got into the cracks and ate away at the rock. The water contained large amounts of **sulfuric acid**, which **dissolved** the rock. The cracks slowly got bigger. After millions of years, the cracks became caves and caverns.

The caves that formed in the limestone have different shapes. Some caves are long and thin. Other caves are very big, with ceilings that are as high as tall buildings. The many different forms of the caves are part of the beauty of Carlsbad Caverns.

*This underground pool is called Atlantis Pool. It is in Lechuguilla Cave in Carlsbad Caverns National Park.*

# Decorated by Drops

Water also formed the shapes that cover the walls, the floors, and the ceilings of Carlsbad Caverns. Water carried **minerals** into the caves, then left them on the walls and the ceilings. Rocks are made of minerals. After many years, the minerals piled up and grew into shapes that look like icicles, curtains, **spikes**, and frozen rivers. The shapes are called **speleothems**.

Some examples of minerals are gold, rubies, and diamonds. The speleothems in Carlsbad Caverns are mostly made of a mineral called **calcite**. Calcite is usually white, but it also can be orange or even clear.

*The caves are covered with speleothems. Some speleothems hang down from the ceiling like icicles. Other formations rise up from the floor, like trees.*

# Entering the Caverns

One of the entrances to Carlsbad Caverns is called the Natural Entrance. Visitors can enter the caverns there, then walk down to the Main Corridor. The Main Corridor leads to the first cavern, which is 829 feet (253 m) below the surface. The air in the caverns is cool, usually staying between 55°F and 60°F (13°C–16°C) all year long.

The first large cavern that visitors see is the Green Lake Room. This room is named for a green-colored pool that is found there. One speleothem in the Green Lake Room is called the Veiled Statue. The Veiled Statue is covered in **flowstone**, which looks like a veil. Flowstone is made of minerals such as calcite. It covers much of the walls and floors in the caverns.

*Visitors to the caverns follow a zigzag route from the Natural Entrance to the Main Corridor.*

# The King's Palace

A little deeper into the caverns is a room called the King's Palace. This part of the caverns was named for all of the fancy speleothems that are found there. There are almost as many decorations in the King's Palace as you might see in a real palace.

Some speleothems hang from the ceiling. These formations are called **stalactites**. One stalactite in the King's Palace is called the King's **Bellcord**. The King's Bellcord is a **soda straw** stalactite that has grown to be 8.5 feet (2.5 m) long.

**Stalagmites** are speleothems that form on the cavern floor. They slowly build up toward the ceiling. When a stalactite and a stalagmite meet, they form a **column**.

*The King's Palace contains many different kinds of stalactites and stalagmites.*

# The Queen's Chamber

Next to the King's Palace is the Queen's Chamber. The Queen's Chamber is smaller than the King's Palace, but it also has many speleothems. **Draperies** are one type of speleothem in the Queen's Chamber. Draperies are made by mineral-rich water that slides along a sloping wall. The mineral in the draperies is calcite. Some of the draperies are **transparent**, which means light can pass through them.

The Queen's Chamber leads to the Papoose Room. *Papoose* is a Native American word for "baby." This small room has hundreds of small stalactites. There are so many stalactites that it almost looks like a porcupine is hanging from the ceiling.

*The draperies in the Queen's Chamber are made of calcite. This bottle brush speleothem is made of the mineral aragonite.*

# The Big Room

The Big Room is deep inside of Carlsbad Caverns. It is the largest natural limestone cavern in the United States. It is 4,000 feet (1,219 m) long and 625 feet (191 m) wide. The highest part of the ceiling is 255 feet (78 m) high.

In the Big Room, there are speleothems called the Totem Poles, Mirror Lake, the Hall of Giants, the Statue of Liberty, and even Santa Claus. These speleothems are named for the objects that they resemble. Another of the speleothems in the Big Room is the Giant **Chandelier**. It hangs down from the middle of the ceiling. It took about 800,000 years for the Giant Chandelier to grow to the size it is today. It grew little by little as drops of water left bits of calcite on the ceiling of the Big Room.

*The Giant Domes are one of the many features to be seen in the Big Room.*

# Pools with Jewels

From the Big Room, a hallway leads to a room called the Lower Cave. In the Lower Cave are shapes called **pisolites**. Pisolites are also known as cave pearls. Pisolites form when dripping water tosses around tiny grains of sand or rock in a small pool. As the grains move around in the water, layers of minerals build up on them.

Another kind of speleothem that forms in pools is called a lily pad. A lily pad forms when drops of water fall into pools and create tiny ripples in the pool. The movement of the water makes it release some of its calcite. The calcite builds up into the shape of a circle or a pad.

*Walking through Carlsbad Caverns is like walking through a maze! Stalactites and stalagmites cover every surface of the caves.*

# Cave Life

Many animals live inside Carlsbad Caverns, including 13 different kinds of bats. In the early evening, thousands of bats fly out of the caverns all at once. They fly into the night sky to hunt for insects. In fact bats were what first interested Jim White, the curious cowboy, in Carlsbad Caverns. From a distance, he thought he saw a tall cloud of smoke coming from a cave. When he got closer, he realized that the cloud was actually a group of bats. Visitors still gather every evening to watch the bats as they fly away.

Jim White was the first person to draw attention to Carlsbad Caverns and its many natural wonders. Thanks to him, every year many visitors come to see the beauty of Carlsbad Caverns.

# Glossary

**bellcord** (BEL-kord)  A rope that is pulled to ring a bell

**calcite** (KAL-syt)  A type of mineral found in limestone.

**caverns** (KA-vurns)  Caves that are large and mostly underground.

**chandelier** (shan-duh-LEER)  A kind of light that hangs from the ceiling.

**column** (KAH-lum)  Something that is tall and thin, like a post or a pillar.

**dissolved** (dih-ZAHLVD)  To seem to disappear when mixed with a liquid.

**draperies** (DRAY-puh-reez)  A type of speleothem made when mineral-rich water slides along the sloping wall of a limestone cave.

**explore** (ik-SPLOR)  To travel through little-known land.

**flowstone** (FLOH-stohn)  A layered deposit of calcite from thin flows of water.

**geographers** (jee-AH-gruh-ferz)  Scientists who study the features of Earth.

**limestone** (LYM-stohn)  A rock that is formed from shells and skeletons.

**minerals** (MIH-ner-ulz)  The natural ingredients that make up almost everything on Earth.

**pisolites** (PIH-suh-lyts)  Types of speleothems that are small and round.

**soda straw** (SOH-da STRAW)  A type of stalagtite.

**spectacular** (spek-TAK-yoo-lur)  Very unusual or impressive.

**speleothems** (SPEE-lee-oh-thimz)  Mineral formations inside of caves.

**spikes** (SPYKS)  Sharp, pointed objects that stick out.

**stalactites** (stuh-LAK-tyts)  Mineral formations that hang down from the ceilings of caves. They can be shaped like icicles.

**stalagmites** (stuh-LAG-myts)  Mineral formations that rise up from the ground.

**sulfuric acid** (suhl-FYUR-ik A-sid)  A chemical element that can eat away solid matter.

**transparent** (tranz-PAYR-ent)  Able to be seen through, or sheer.

# Index

# Web Sites

To find out more about Carlsbad Caverns, check out these Web sites:
www.americansouthwest.net/new_mexico/carlsbad_caverns/
national_park.html
www.desertusa.com/carl/